TANDEM

The Bedsid

The Milliside Bedman

The Sideigan Millibed

The Millside Bedagain

The Milligad Bedsign

Whichever way you put it this book can be dipped
into at any suitable interval and you may come out
with an uproarious lump, a lump in the throat,
or a thoughtful lump.
Whichever it is it will be beneficial, or so say the
publishers from experience.

so

BUY THIS BOOK
IT'S GOOD FOR YOU
AND ANYBODY ELSE
But for God's sake buy it!
*PUBLISHER'S NOTE
*IN FACT EVERY NOTE

Also by Spike Milligan

A DUSTBIN OF MILLIGAN
    Tandem edition 25p

A BOOK OF BITS or A BIT OF A BOOK
    Tandem edition 25p

THE LITTLE POT-BOILER
    Tandem edition 25p

By Spike Milligan and
John Antrobus

THE BEDSITTING ROOM
    Tandem edition 25p

The Bedside Milligan

OR READ YOUR WAY TO INSOMNIA

Spike Milligan

with guest appearance by
Margaret and Jack Hobbs

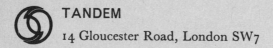 TANDEM
14 Gloucester Road, London SW7

First published in Great Britain by
Margaret and Jack Hobbs, 1969
Published by Universal-Tandem Publishing Co. Ltd, 1971
Reprinted October 1971
Reprinted July 1972
Reprinted February 1973
Reprinted September 1973

Printed in Great Britain by The Anchor Press Ltd.,
and bound by Wm. Brendon & Son Ltd.,
both of Tiptree, Essex

A GNOTE

Walk round to the back of this book. There you will find a picture of a GNU marked '10 o'clock Gnus'. Take a pencil and draw a clock on the body of the GNU with the small hand pointing to the 10 and the large hand pointing to the 12. And then it all happens.

THE SINGING FOOT (A tale of a singing foot)

Woy Woy, Australia.
September 1967.

I have an Uncle. His name is Herbert Jam.
He was 52. He worked in a laundry. One
Christmas Eve he was homeward bound on a
crowded bus when he heard what he thought
was the sound of music coming from inside
his boot; indeed, what was to make him famous
had happened, his right foot had commenced
to sing. Poor Mr. Jam tried to control the
volume of sound by tightening his boot lace;
it only succeeded in making the voice go
from a deep baritone to a strangled tenor.
At the next stop Mr. Jam had to get off. He
walked home to the sound of his right foot
singing 'God rest you merry gentlemen',
fortunately, Mr. Jam knew the words and
mimed them whenever people passed by.
It was all very, very embarrassing. For three
days he stayed off work. His favourite T.V.
programmes were ruined by unexpected bursts
of song from the foot, he did manage to
deaden it by watching with his foot in a bucket
of sand, but, alas, from this practice he
contracted a rare foot rot normally only
caught by Arabs and camels. Worst was to
come. The foot started singing at night. At
three in the morning he was awakened with

selections from 'The Gondoliers', 'Drake is going West' and 'A Whiter Shade of Pale'. He tried Mrs. Helen Furg, a lady who was known to have exorcised Poltergeists and Evil Spirits, she tried a sprig of witchhazel round his ankle, intoned druidic prayers and burnt all his socks in the bath, but it wasn't long before the strains of 'The Desert Song' came lilting up his trouser leg again. On the recommendation of his doctor he visited the great Harley Street right-foot specialist, Sir Ralph Fees.

"Come in, sit down," said the great man, "Now what appears to be our trouble?"

"It's my right foot."

"Of course it is" said cheery Sir Ralph "and" he went on "what appears to be the trouble with our right foot?"

"It sings."

Sir Ralph paused (but still went on charging) "You say your foot sings?"

"Yes, it's a light baritone" said wretched Jam. Sir Ralph started to write. "I want you to go and see this Psychiatrist" he said—at which very moment Uncle Herbert's foot burst into song! "Just a minute" said Sir Ralph "I'll get my hat and come with you." The medical world and Harley Street were baffled. For the time he had to make do with a surgical sound-proof boot and a pair of wax ear-plugs. Occasionally, he would take off his boot to give the lads at the Pub a song, but, Mr. Jam was far from happy. Then came the beginning of the end, E.M.I. gave him a £500,000,000 contract for his foot to make records. A special group was formed, called 'The Grave', the billing was 'Mr. Jam with One Foot in the Grave'. He was the news sensation of the year! But, it became clear that it was the right foot that got the fame, not Mr. Jam. E.M.I. opened a bank account for the right foot. While his poor left foot wore an old boot his right foot wore expensive purple alligator shoes from Carnaby Street which cost £50 a toe. At parties he was ceaselessly taking off his shoe to sign autographs! Mr. Jam was just an embarrassment to his right foot! One night in a fit of jealousy Mr. Jam shot his foot through the instep. It never sang again! Mr. Jam returned to the obscurity of his job in the laundry. He was 52, happy, only now he walked with a slight limp.

Rabbits they say
Are very scarce to-day
My diagnosis?
Myxamatousis.

NON RABBIT
ELEPHANT.

Terence Newt
Wore a Giant boot
Jammed down over his head
And he kept it there
~~with another care~~ {with his ears and Chair}
Until the day he was dead.
But when his wife removed the boot,
She discovered to her horror!
It was not the head of Terence Newt
But three other men. Tom Daft an apprentice
butcher, Cyril hunge a Mechanic and Arthur Woggs. Dentist.

Terence Newt
Wore a giant boot
Jammed down over his head
And he kept it there
With his ears and hair
Until the day he was dead.
But when his wife removed the boot,
She discovered to her horror!
It was not the head of Terence Newt
But three other men. Tom Daft an apprentice
butcher, Cyril Lunge a Mechanic, and
Arthur Woggs, Dentist.

Hopeless Love

It is a Hopeless time.
You are spring
And I —
Am Autumn.
Love can't close the gap.
And if it could — if it did —
One day you will be Autumn
And I Winter — and after that?

Midnight
Bournemouth
April 1967

A Boarding Home
in Christchurch Rd

The Jet Plane —!
Brilliant — time saving
The new Icarus — with Tangled Wings
And for me —
it just takes me from one unhappiness to another —
tis another

The Young Soldiers

Why are they lying in some distant land
Why did they go, did they understand?
Young men they were
Young men they stay
But why did we send them away, away?

written during Korean War
March 30th 1955

Got a Picture of a Gnu.
Cut it out. place it over a
news paper. Caption. The
10 o'clock Gnus.

Christmas Morning

A little girl called Silé Javotte
Said 'Look at the lovely presents I've got'.
A little girl in Biafra said
'Oh! What a lovely slice of bread.

Samson and Delilah

As he pushed the pillars apart
Samson was appalled
For just before the palace fell in
Delilah said 'He's bald!'.

Time Gentlemen

A.tick. A.tock.
Goes grandfather clock,
All through the night.
And. every hour
With tremendous power
The clock would start to chime..

And may,
I say,
Its a noisy way,
For it,
to tell,
the Time.

A Nose
A World War II Nose

My nose, my nose lived dangerously
Its courage was no stunt!
And during the war in Germany
It was always out in front!

Yet when the battle was o'er
And we'd defeated the Hun
Suddenly, for no reason at all
My nose started to run.

These things called

The human face is something that
Hangs downwards from a thing called hat
And when the hat is raised, it's said
It shows a hairy thing called head.
Now I would rather cover face
And strike it full on with a mace.

Mermaid Theatre.   20 Dec. 1967

Brave New World

Twinkle Twinkle, little star
How I wonder what you are
Up above the sky so high
Like a almond in the sky

Twinkle Twinkle, little star
I've just found out what you are
A lump of rusting rocket case
A rubbish tip - in outer space.

Dear Reader!

Dublin
Nov. 1967

Human beings will become so used to being crushed together that when they are on their own, they will suffer withdrawal symptoms. "Doctor—I've got to get into a crowded train soon or I'll go mad". So, special N.H.S. assimilated rush hour trains will be run every other Sunday for patients. At 9 o'clock on that morning, thousands of victims will crowd platforms throughout England, where great electrically powered Crowd Compressors will crush hundreds of writhing humans into trains, until their eyes stand out under the strain, then, even more wretches are forced in by smearing them with vaseline and sliding them in sideways between legs of standing passengers. The doors close—any bits of clothing, ears or fingers are snipped off. To add to the sufferers' relief great clouds of stale cigarette smoke are pumped into the carriages. The patients start to cough, laugh and talk. They're feeling better already. But more happiness is on the way. The train reaches 80 m.p.h., at the next station the driver slams the brakes on shooting all the victims up to one end of the carriages. Immediately the doors open, and great compressed air tubes loaded with up to 100 passengers are fired into the empty spaces, this goes on until the rubber roofs of the carriages give upwards, and the lumps you see are yet a second layer of grateful patients. Off goes the train, and one sees the relief on the travellers' faces. Who wants LSD when you can get this? Ah! you say, the train can't possibly take any more. Wrong! At the next stop the train is sprayed with a powerful adhesive glue, and fresh passengers stuck to the outside, and so, crushed to pulp, pop-eyed and coughing blood, the train carries out its work of mercy. Those who are worried about their children's future in the 20th century need not fear. We are prepared.

Mr. Timothy Pringle
Lived on his own
As he was single.
Returning from work
In the evening gloom
He found an elephant
In his room.
It had a label
Round its neck
"My name is Doris
Eileen Beck".
Even if the name was Jim
It didn't really help poor Tim.
Is that elephant a her or he?
Asked Mr. Screws (the landlady)
Tim said "It's a female elephant, why?"
"No women in rooms" was the stern reply.

Mr Timothy Pringle
Lived on his own
As he was single.
Returning from work
In the evening gloom
He found an Elephant
In his room
It had a $label)
Round its neck
"My name is Doris
Eileen Beck".
Even if the name.Jim
It didn't really help poor Tim.
Is that Elephant a her or he?
Asked Mr Screws [his landlady]
Tim said Its a female elephant why?
'No women in rooms' was the stern reply

Pass by Citizen:
   don't look left or right,
keep those drip dry eyes straight ahead.
A tree? Chop it down.
      they're a danger to lightning
Pansies, calling for water?
      Let 'em die — the queer bastards!
Seek comfort in the scarlet plastic
        labour saving rose
Fresh with the fragrance of Daz.
Sunday. Pray citizen:
   pray that no rain will fall
    on your newly polished
       four wheeled
        God.

Envoi. Beauty is in the eye of the beholder. Get it out — with Optrex.

On a train to Liverpool, Easter Monday 1967.

Phillip le Barr
Was knocked down by a car
On the road to Mandalay
He was knocked down again
By a dust cart in Spain
And again, in Zanzibar
So,
He travelled at night
In the pale moon-light
Away from the traffic's growl
But terrible luck
He was hit by a duck
Driven by — an owl.

Little tiny puppy dog
Sleeping soundly as a log
Better wake him for his dinner
Or else he'll start to sleep much thinner.

3rd of Sliptimber
The Olleth of Arg

Dear Reader,

At last I've completed my first reliable
Leaping Stone. This Stone is a simple method
of forcing oneself to leap and as a result
become quite an expert, the best places to
place these stones are (1) Halfway up the
stairs—in the Centre of the Bathroom door—
or in the middle of the front garden gate. The
stone—roughly the shape of an old Grave
stone, should be wide enough to block a
passage around it, and 3 ft. 2 in. high. Once
a client has shown interest in leaping stones
several demonstration stones should be
cemented into his house—one in every door
in fact, a Leapo-meter is attached to the ankle
of every member of the family, which records
the number of leaps per person, per day,
per-haps. Those who show disinterest can
have a small explosive charge fixed to the
groin, which detonates should the person try
climbing round these stones, this will cause
many a smoke blackened crutch, but with our
new spray-on 'Crutcho'—a few squirts leave
the groins gleaming white and free of foul-
pest. Think of the enervating joys of the
Leaping stones! Sunday morn—and the whole

household rings with shouts of Hoi Hup!
Ho la! Grannies—uncles—Mothers—cripples
—all leaping merrily from one room to another
—ah, there's true happiness. We have high
hopes that more progressive young politicians
with an eye to eliminating senile M.P.s, intend
to have a 'Great Westminster Leaping Stone'
that will be placed dead centre of the Great
entrance doors on the opening day of
Parliament—those failing will of course
be debarred—though they can claim 'A
brethren assisted leap'—this means that two
decrepit M.P.s of the same party, can try and
assist the failed member over the leaping
stone by applying hot pokers to the seat, thus
the smell of scorched seats, burning hairs
and screams, can bring a touch of colour
to an otherwise dull occasion. I don't know
when I will post this letter, I might deliver it
tomorrow by hand, ankle, foot and clenched
elbow.

As ever,
Spike.

It's in
here
somewhere

(23)

Oh the Wiggley-Woggley men
They don't get up till ten
They run about
Then give shout
And go back to bed again!

Oh the Wiggley-Woggley men
They don't get up till ten
They run about
Then give a shout
And back to bed again!

An Ear passed me
   the other day
And silently
   went on its way

I wonder who
   that ear can be
And has it ever
   heard of me.

Manic Depression

St. Lukes Wing
Woodside Hospital
Psychiatric Wing   1953 - 4

The pain is too much
A thousand grim winters
   grow in my head.
In my ears
   the sound of the
      coming dead
All seasons, all same
   all living
   all pain
No opiate to lock still
   my senses.
Only left, the body locked tenser.

December 1960.

Manic Depression

The pain is too much
A thousand grim winters
        grow in my head.

In my ears
        the sound of the
            coming dead

All seasons, all same
        all living
        all pain

No opiate to lock still
            my senses.

Only left, the body locked tenses.

37

Norrington Blitt
Ate aught but grit
Ate aught but grit and mussels
But when he got there
The cupboard was bare
Save a sack of sprouts —
From Brussels, or was it Oldham?
No — a tree fell on him.
Or was —

Freedom

A bird in flight,
　　her wings spread wide
Is the soul of man
　　with bonds untied
Beyond the plough
　　the spade, the God
A bird flies in
　　the face of God,

　Yet I with reason
　　bright as day
　Forever tread
　　the earthbound clay.

PARIS PAREE

Written in Paris when
I went last time.

Paris! Paree! What pictures of gaiety those
two cities conjour up, down, and sideways,
Paris, city of Napoleon, the Revolution, the
Mob, the blood, the head rolling. Alas, those
happy days are gone, yet, Paris, the Queen of
cities calls us all. Last week it called me,
'Cooee!' it said and I responded. Travel
allowance being only £50, I saved by taking
sandwiches and a Thermos of Tomato Sauce.
I saved further on the air fare by travelling
second class non-return tourist night flight,
all you had to do was sign a Secret Enoch
Powell form saying you were an undesirable
coloured alien with uncurable bed-wetting.
At the airport there was the carefully disguised
panic rush to get the back seats in the plane.
On take-off I fastened my safety belt, read
'How to inflate Life Belt', swallowed a boiled
sweet, made the sign of the cross and read
the Times. One hour later coming in to Orly I
fastened my copy of the Times, made the sign
of the seat belt, swallowed my boiled life belt
and inflated myself for landing. Through to
Customs and out! At the airport my taxi
drew up in a cloud of Garlic, and the driver
leapt out and gesticulated in a corner.

Arriving at the Hotel, the porter raised his hat and lowered his trousers. Real French hospitality! The Hotel had been built in 1803—in 1804 they added a west wing and in 1819 it flew away. Next morning I was up at the crack of noon shouting "Apres moi le deluge" and whistling Toulouse Lautrec, I hurriedly swallowed a breakfast of porridge and frogs and a steaming bidet of coffee. I next joined a crowd of impoverished British tourists on the 30 centimes all-in English punishment Tour. A great herd of us assembled at the Place du Concord, from there we were force-marched to the Notre Dame, beaten with sticks and made to climb the great Bell Tower. Sheer physical agony! On the way up we passed many who had perished in the attempt and never made it. Fancy! 600 steps! No wonder Quasi Modo had a hump on his back when he got to the top! From the top I took several lovely photos of the Eiffel Tower. At Midday, we were led to a Cafe 'Le Gogo Plastique', the establishment bore the indelible stamp of the British tourists—

Menu

'Escargots and mash . . .'
'Bisque d'Homard, bread and butter'
'Pate de Fois Gras and Chips'
'Lobster Thermidor, 2 Veg., Boiled Pots. etc.'
'Crepe Suzette Flambe and Custard'

The lady next to me had Frogs' legs, her friend's weren't much better. It's all that walking, I suppose. I was served by a waiter who made it perfectly clear he held me personally responsible for a) The loss of Algeria b) Waterloo c) Edith Piaff. Just so they didn't think I was an oaf, I ordered the whole meal in French—I was brought a hip-bath, a silk tie, a coloured pencil and a small clockwork Virgin Mary that whistled Ave Maria every hour, made in Hong Kong. I spent the rest of the afternoon sketching the beautiful Eiffel Tower. There's always something to do in Paris! Carefully following my Baedecker's Paris I walked up the hill to the Cemetery of Pierre Lachaze, I saw the very spot where Moulin Rouge lay buried, and above me gleaming white was the Sacred Cur, now used as a church. I had been walking some three hours and as a quick calculation showed me that I was exactly six miles from the lovely Eiffel Tower, I took a taxi back to the Pension; to my horror he asked for 13 francs, I was about to have a show down with him, but, rather than ruin the evening, I paid him. It ruined the evening. I freshened up in my room, taking a shower and a foot-bath in a very low basin with a rather dangerous water jet that took me completely by surprise. The evening would be dedicated to Art, I always wanted to see the French Impressionists so I booked for the Folie Bergere where a man was doing imitations of Maurice Chevalier, Josephine Baker, and many others. What a show! Women uncovered from the waist up, and yet there was a cover charge! Watching women with naked bosoms is unsettling, but eventually they grow on you. If they grew on me I'd go to the pictures alone. The Grand Finale was called 'Salute les Anglais', the band played a Pop version of God Save the Queen while a French queer wearing a Prince Philip mask juggled with three Plastic Busts of the heir presumptive. It was good to see that we were still a country to be respected. If only we had their Eiffel Tower there'd be no stopping us.

29

Painted in 1866

(canvas 11″ × 16″)

Blot on the Landscape

George Melley
Had such a fat Belly
He couldn't get near the Telly
So he had to go
And listen to the Radio.

All the ravel-avel tumble-umblings — all the high sorrows —
All going all giving all taking all doing. Which, what
When where how — worse still. Who? Who's next? —
I know — it's me — it's always me; time for it now sir —
Now son — now — now — NOW it's time for it. Yes.
Now the drop down starts — sitting, standing, kneeling
Lying — the drop starts — down down — it's always down —
Some time down stops — but it only stops at down — then
Off it goes again — down, down, down, into the unanswerable.

Over Elba — September, 1967.
Drunk

Skeleton of Prehistoric Car

Bronta cycle

Said the mother Tern
     to her baby Tern
Would you like a brother?
Said baby Tern
     to mother Tern
Yes
One good Tern deserves another.

Sent to Chiselhurst & Sidcup College.

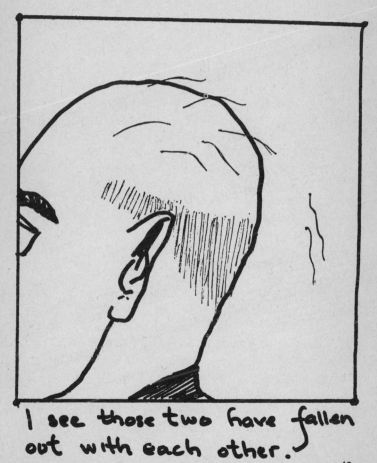

I see those two have fallen out with each other.

9 Orme Court,
Bayswater,
W.2.
13 June, 1963.

Sir,
     Whereas the Bishop of Southwark is to
be complimented on his speech (Times,
13 June '63) when he speaks of "corruption
in high places", what he should have said
was "corruption in all places". To point the
finger of indictment at one or two persons,
is almost laughable when one considers the
extent of moral corruption in this country
as a whole, and this corruption feeds on the
licence it is allowed by the feeble Church
and Parliamentary laws, which almost condone
it. Pornography, which is the greatest inciter
of immorality, is not only rife, but actually
bestowed, in some spheres, as 'art', by the
intellectuals, which is quickly exploited by all
commercial enterprises. Films of rape, murder,
sex, debasement, are now 'la mode', to criticise
them is to be 'old hat'. The X certificate is
box-office bonanza. Even innocent comedies
have publicity that is aimed at sex. As a
parent, I find it increasingly difficult to take
my children to see a suitable film. Bookstalls
in all our major cities groan under the weight
of pornographic 'literature', Men's 'clubs'
doing nothing but strip-shows, drinking
cluhs show films that are laughingly called

'Naked but free' etc., etc. Photographic pornography, using safe Box numbers, is a million pound trade. In the light of this I fear Dr. Stockwood's address will have little or no effect at all, yet, it is in religious laxity that the seeds of immorality grow, and, at this critical stage in history, never has the Christian church been so inactive and indifferent to the massive danger to Christianity. Take China as an example, the Christians were in China 500 years before Communism. Today in China, Christianity hardly exists, why? Parrot-indoctrination; give the native a vest, a crucifix, one chorus of 'Onward Christian Soldiers', and he's ticked off as being a Christian, and still Christians are churned out as tho' from a mould, size is no substitute for quality. I myself was baptised a Catholic, and I still don't know what it is all about, nobody ever bothered to teach me. Year after year I listen for a message of enlightenment from the pulpit, but no, the Gospels, the Epistles, are repeated ad nauseum, but of contemporary guidance there is nothing. Going round saying "And the Lord said unto Moses" won't get us anywhere, Jesus didn't talk about throwing the money lenders out of the Temple, he did it, then talked. If we are to stop the moral rot, we must act, we must indict, we must mention the offenders by name and not hide for fear of libel, the truth is all that matters, right now this country is not geared to accept it.

Consider, that England, France, Italy, West
Germany and America are where pornography
abounds, and these are the countries dedicated
to preserve Christianity from the Godless
Russia who has no pornography.
                              Spike Milligan

A little poem for Sean

There was a young boy called Sean
Who sat on the edge of a lawn
His knees went crack!
He fell on his back
And regretted the day he was born.

I sent my legs out for a walk
To keep them strong and fit
They would not go without me
So I've made the b . . . . . s sit.

THINK OF THE MONEY YOU'LL SAVE IN TRANSPORT.

Cautionary Letter

Green Bonk

Dear reader, the worst has happened. Brown
Bonk has struck in the Quantocks. Worse
still, attacks of Green Bonk have been reported
coming from the Urals; an Armenian fruit
shepherd was driving a herd of Apple trees
to water when the Brown Bonk laid him low.
The first case of our own Brown Bonk was at
Catford Labour Exchange. Mr. Ted Naffs was
being given his certificate for 21 years of
devoted unemployment, when, yes! Brown
Bonk! Smoke started to issue from Mr. Naffs'
mouth, a scream of agony showed his teeth
to be molten white. He was rushed to a
blacksmith who removed his ring of
confidence. Toothless with Brown Bonk, Mr.
Naffs was given a pair of N.H.S. electric teeth,
for high speed eating, a boon to the aged
and infirm. Leave the food and teeth by your
bed at night and they do your eating while
you sleep. Alas, Mr. Naffs' house, was all
Gas. An application had to be made for a set
of North Sea High Speed Gas-operated Teeth.
While he was waiting for delivery Mr. Naffs
stupidly plugged into the great overhead
cables of the National Electric grid which ran
over his cottage. As he switched on

100,000,000 volts shot into his 240 volt teeth, a brilliant flash of magnesium, and his dentures' started to chew at round about the speed of light, Mr. Naffs' head became a white blurr as his teeth ate the porridge—the plate—knife —fork—spoon—table mat—the table—the chairs—the dog—the cat—two budgies—a Welsh dresser, he was half way through a brick wall when the annual power failure saved him. Beware all of you, Brown Bonk is with us, at the first sign of smouldering teeth. . . . . Write to the fire brigade.

I had a Dongee
Who would not speak
He wouldn't hop
He would'nt creep
He would'nt walk.
He would'nt leap
He would'nt wake
He would'nt sleep
He would'nt shout
He would'nt squeak
He would'nt look
He would'nt peep
He would'nt wag
     his Dongee tail.
I think this Dongees
          going to fail.

If Robert Graves
   misbehaves
It's the Torjca
   Majorca

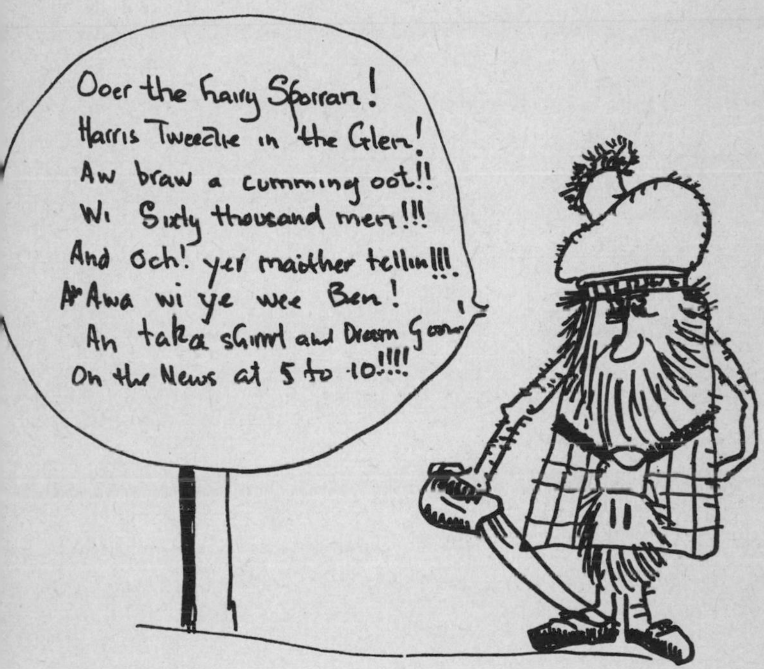

The sayings of Mrs. Doris Reach
of 23 The Irons, Cleethorpes, Herts.

1. Ups a Daisy
2. Save the string.
3. There's some in the tin on the Mantlepiece.
4. They should never let them in the country.
5. Ups a Daisy
6. I had an Aunt who was like that.
7. Mine's Brown.
8. Just a small one then.
9. Ups a Daisy.
10. It comes off with Turps.
11. He knows every word you say.
12. Ups a Daisy.
13. What about a nice. . . . .
14. Ups a Daisy.

Editor. Rag Mag., Gloucester College of
Education.

You say your mag. is in aid of mental health!
Dear Lad, there's no such thing, if there was
anybody in position of power with any
semblance of mental health do you think the
world would be in this bloody mess? Young
minds at risk is different. Anybody with a
young mind is taking a risk—young means
fresh—unsullied, ready to be gobbled up in an
adult world bringing the young into visionless
world of adults, like all our leaders. Their
world is dead—dead—dead, and my God,
that's why it stinks! They look at youth in
horror—and say 'They are having a revolution',
but what do they want? I say they don't
know what they want, but they know what
they don't want, and that is, the repetition of
the past mistakes, towards which the adult
old order is still heading. War—armistice—
building up to pre-war standards—
capitalism—labour—crisis—war and so on.
I digress.
Mental Health. I have had five nervous
breakdowns—and all the medics gave me was
medicine—tablets—but no love or any attempt
at involvement, in this respect I might as well
have been a fish in a bowl. The mentally ill

need LOVE, UNDERSTANDING—
TOLERANCE, as yet unobtainable on the
N.H.S. or the private world of psychiatry, but
tablets, yes, and a bill for £5 5. 0. a visit—if
they know who you are it's £10 10. 0. a visit
—the increased fee has an immediate
depressing effect—so you come out worse
than you went in.
As yet, I have not been cured, patched up
via chemicals, yes. Letter unfinished, but
I've run out of time—sorry!

Regards,
Spike

Once there was a girl
Who grew roses in my head
Made a paradise of bed
Yet not a word was said.

My Street

Pass by
Pull the blinds
Nothing happened here to-day

Douse the light
    lock the door.

      Nothings happened.

Walk the street
    turn the corner
       Nothing there. forever more

What was it -
so quick.
So Unthought
Yet - Alright
It was'nt me
It was'nt you
Yet it was —
Before "
After "
During
We were looking
for the
answer to
one plus one

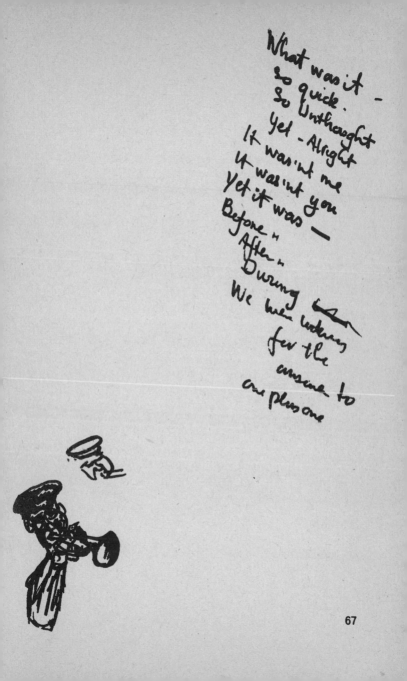

What was it –
So quick
So Unthought
Yet – all right?
It wasn't me
or you –
then – it was
Before –
After
During – supply the same
We we just all the answer

Penne Scales Club

68

What was it?
So quick
So unthought
Yet — Alright
It wasn't me
It wasn't you
Yet it was —
Before
  After
    During.

We were looking for the
answer to one plus one.

Ronnie Scotts Club.

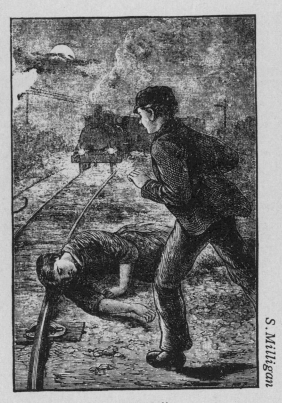

S. Milligan

"No, no, try ASPIRIN."

Dear Lads,

I am so overwhelmed with work at the moment, and by this, I don't mean the sheer monetary kind: I also try and have an interest in humanity.

Anyhow, I just haven't got time for an article. However! I would like to state that I have been aware of the coming dissent among students for the last ten years against a world, which has become archaic in ideas, and the extension of those ideas.

The normal channels left open to citizens to complain are crammed to the brink, and normally no individual citizen can get anything changed under the present system, unless he is willing to spend £10,000 and go to litigation, that, or set fire to himself outside No. 10 Downing Street, which would, in turn, only result in a bucket of water from the Prime Minister.

Whereas, students are not at all clear as to what they want, they certainly know what they don't want.

The old world and its standard formula of democracy are spent forces, who can only go on repeating past mistakes on the same democratic basis, among these we have over-population, starvation, war, political unrest, and archaic laws which themselves are evil. One only has to investigate the modern divorce law to discover to what disgusting levels human beings are reduced, to obtain a divorce.

Religion has become unchristian, the Christ that lived would certainly look extremely embarrassed and out of place in the Vatican. Christian morals have changed to such an extent that people are now on the verge of accepting debasement as some form of art. Jesus chose a donkey. Top clergy use Austin Princesses!

I myself am not a prude, but I am finding it difficult to find a film, a book, or a magazine that does not use the sex act as the basis of world art form.

All this is being seen very clearly by student bodies around the world, and through the extraordinary combustion exploding at the same time.

Unfortunately, the old guard are so firmly entrenched and the system so protected by armed forces, police and lackies, that only civil war can bring about a change.

Modern student thinking is violently opposed to the use of arms (or at least it should be), but student bodies must keep up the pressure for the rest of their lives to try and influence their wives, and children and children's children into thinking of a new method for man to live on this earth. Governments can start by solving the most important problem in the world, over-population, which in itself leads to the lowering of all man's standards.

I haven't time to say much more, but let us say that the old world has got to change, and by the old world I also mean these idiots who want to get to the moon, when man hasn't really got to the earth.

Sincerely,
Spike Milligan

P.S. I keep fighting.

Its little God,

When my daddys in the bath
I knock upon the door
'Whos dat' he says
But I dont say and then?
I knock some <u>more</u>,
Whos dad 'hes says' Whos dat again?
And he must think its odd
For when at last I answer him
'Its me' I say " Its God!"

He swung to and fro
Then   3 and fro
         4 and fro
         5 and fro
And finally 6 and fro.

SUN HELMET

A pleasant three degrees below zero wind
was blowing. The early morning Londoners
shivered through the bitingly cold rush hour.
Among them was a bowler-hatted Mr. Oliver
Thrigg. The first snow of summer was starting
to fall as he joined his 'AA members only'
bus cue. Glancing to a bus que opposite (it
was a different que to his cue, as the spelling
proves), and what he saw shook him to his
foundation garment. There, in the que opposite,
was a man wearing a sun helmet, eccentricity
yes, but this fellow didn't have a stamp of
a genuine eccentric, no, fellow looked far too
normal! Curiosity got the upper hand, crossing
the road he killed a cat. Once across he
joined the que and left his on the other side.
The man in the sun-helmeted man caught a
31A bus, Mr. Thrigg signalled a passing
49A. "Follow that bus" he told the driver.
"Anywhere but Cuba" said the driver. At
Victoria Station the sun-helmeted man booked
to Southampton, as did Mr. Thrigg, who kept
him under surveyaliance until they reached
Southampton, where by now the snow was
3 foot deep, which explained the absence of

dwarfs in the street. The man continued to wear his sun helmet. "Why, Why, Why" said Thrigg whose curiosity had killed another nine cats, making a grand total of one. "I must follow this man etc." The man booked aboard the Onion Castle and was handed £10 and an oar (Assisted Passage they call it). The ship headed south, and, so did Mr. Thrigg and his enigma, which he used for colonic irrigation. During the whole trip the man appeared at all times in a sun helmet. Several or eightal times he was almost tempted to ask the man his secret. But no, as Thrigg was travelling steerage and the man 1st Class, plus the fact it was a special Non-fraternising Apartheid Cruise, no contact was possible. On the 12th of Iptomber the ship docked at Cape Town. Even though Thrigg got through Customs and Bribes at speed, he just missed the Sun Helmet as he drove off in a taxi. Thrigg flagged down an old cripple Negro driver "Follow that Sun Helmet" he said jumping on the nigger's back. (The change from Negro to Nigger denotes change from UK to SA soil.) Several times Thrigg let the nigger stand in his bucket of portable UK soil so he could be called Negro. To cut the story short, Mr. Thrigg used scissors and cornered the man in the middle of the Sahara. The heat was intolerable as Thrigg walked up and said "Why are you wearing that sun helmet?" "Because said the man, pointing at a 113° thermometer in the shade "The sun man! This protects

the head." "I see" said Mr. Thrigg. "Well I
better be off, I'm late for work." As he
departed for the caravan que, the man in the
sun helmet spotted him. "Good God, a man
wearing a bowler hat! A bowler hat? Here, in
the Sahara? I must find out why," he thought
as he joined the caravan cue behind Mr.
Thrigg.

Titikaka

The magic green lake
that fell from the sky,
quenched a burning mountain's throat
and sent a fire king
into untimeable slumber.

On a plane over Mexico. Sept. 1968.

Morning

Chamfers of White
        Light
Shaft from the cheap 20th Century glass
Flared on my bed
        Red
Blanket barks its reflection to the ear in
              my eye

And so it
        bit
By bit pulls together the strings of morning.

January 4 at 'Old Place'

lashing - man

At the third stroke
it will be 3.29

The 12th June
is very soon
for there is a party on that Day
and most likly I be going away.

Silue..
June 67

The 18th June
Is very soon
For there is a party
    on that day
And most likely I be
    going away.

                        Silé.   June 1967

A bottle of Graves
              or Graves
I ordered in half
              or halves

How teeny teeny wee
Is the teeny little flea.
But last night in my hotel
He made me scratch like merry hell!

Sir:

I have the honour to acknowledge the
receipt of your Note of the 19th instant,
in which you transmit a copy of your
Credentials as Special Envoy from the
Argentine Republic on the occasion of the
celebration of the Sixtieth Anniversary of
the Queen's Accession to the Throne.

I have the honour to be,
with the highest consideration,
Sir,
Your most obedient
humble servant,

(FOR THE MARQUIS OF SALISBURY)
F. H. Villier

Monsieur Florencio Dominguez
&c., &c., &c.

THE TALE OF FRANCIS PAW

by Margaret and Jack Hobbs

There was a cat called Francis Paw
Who lived behind the kitchen door
He was old and brown
And tumbledown
But his fur was long and silky
He liked an egg for breakfast
And some tea if it was milky.

He often sat in an old silk hat
And talked to me of this and that
He liked a joke
And his voice would croak
As he told me of his youth.

He used to croon
To the harvest moon
And sing a roundelay
Of his Uncle Fred
Who is long since dead
Who went to Botany Bay.

He went aboard a whaling boat
Which foundered in a gale
With feline craft
He clung to a raft
With the end of his scraggy tail.

At last he reached an island fair
And struggled to the shore
Where under a tree
Stood Sam Macgee
Staring at Frederick Paw.

'Yo Ho' he cried
'The cook has died
'What can we have to eat?'
'You look a tasty morsel, lad,
'Except for your smelly feet.'

Fred's ears went flat
'I'll catch a rat'
He said in trembling tones
There isn't very much of me
I'm only skin and bones.

'I would' said Sam
'Prefer a ham'
But I'll give you an hour
To catch a rat that's big and fat
And cook it rolled in flour.

Fred caught a rat
And that was that
And rescue soon was nigh
In the shape of a Chinese sailor
By the name of Wun Flung Hi.

Wun Flung Hi
Had a drooping eye
And a most unsavoury crew
They hit poor Fred
And Sam on the head
And put 'em in Hold No. 2.

They sat in the hold
Through the long dark night
Wondering what to do
When the hatch was raised
And down there gazed
The face of Fu Manchu.

Fu Manchu was a prisoner too
For a ransom so they say
But he'd opened the lock
With a piece of a clock
And planned a getaway.

Fred and Sam and Fu Manchu
Took a boat and sailed away.
And when the dawn
Of the day was born
They landed at Botany Bay.

What happened then
I chose to ask
Of my friend, young Francis Paw
That's another tale
He yawned and fell
Asleep by the kitchen door.

A DUSTBIN OF MILLIGAN

Spike Milligan

If you can't afford a dustbin, folks, buy this!

'My son has asked me to write the "blurb" for this book. What can I say? When he was a lad, he showed a natural inclination to write so I sent him to Eton, and by the time he was 21 he had mastered the Alphabet. He took to travelling everywhere by pram—said it made him look younger. In 1940 he was invited to join World War II (with an option on World War III). Partly out of his mind, he accepted. So, with one stroke of a pen, he put three years on the war, eight on Churchill and twopence on the rates. Oh, how we laughed.'

(signed)   *Dad Milligan*
Orange Grove Road,
Woy Woy,
Orstrilia.

25p

A BOOK OF BITS
OR
A BIT OF A BOOK

Spike Milligan

A BOOK OF BITS or A BIT OF A BOOK is more than a 'Bit of a Book' and not just a Book of Bits.

On the other hand, it is not a bitty book, and it has its 'booky' bits. However . . . it really is impossible to describe a Spike Milligan opus, but if you have read *The Little Pot Boiler* and *A Dustbin of Milligan* this is the book for you (and it's for you even if you haven't).

25p

Name...

Address...

Titles required...

....

....

....

....

....

....

....

- -

The publishers hope that you enjoyed this book and invite you
to write for the full list of Tandem titles.

If you find any difficulty in obtaining these books from your
usual retailer we shall be pleased to supply the titles of your
choice—packing and postage 5p—upon receipt of your
remittance.

write now to:
      Universal-Tandem Publishing Co. Ltd.,
      14 Gloucester Road,
      London SW7 4RD